LOVE IST~
FORCEINTIT v····
WHO CAN EXPLAIN IT ?
ENJOY THE FORCE —

Love Thoughts

HAPPY LOVE THOUGHTS
ALWAY'S

Glenn

g

Love Thoughts

Poems

Glenn Smith

Library of Congress Number:		2004195387
ISBN :	Hardcover	1-4134-8106-X
	Softcover	1-4134-8105-1

To order additional copies of this book, contact:
Xlibris Corporation
1-888-795-4274
www.Xlibris.com
Orders@Xlibris.com
26889

CONTENTS

Love Thoughts 1

Love Thoughts 2

BOY MEETS GIRL

AND HEARTS BURST

MAN MEETS WOMAN

AND THE UNIVERSE TREMBLES . . .

For everyone who has known
The magical union known as love
Hearts and flowers
Flesh and flame
Spring showers
And gentle rains

I dedicate these love thoughts . . .

Love Thoughts 1

When

When did I first know
You were here
In the universe with me
When the stars came out at night
Doing their silent twinkle
Leaving soft glowing light
Giving rapture to my soul

When the moon of moon children
Brought the tides crashing
With tidal waves of change
And leaving the anvil shores
Of my life
Changed for evermore

When the dawn broke
From a sleepless night of joy
Caressing my racing thoughts of you
Charging into, seizing the new day
Of possibilities with you

When all of nature
Sings with joy
And leaves my peasant soul
Crying for more
Of anthems to sing with winds
Clouds and rainbows
And all the birds of creations choir

When your fingers magic played tunes on my eager body
Penetrating my deepest pain
Quenching my thirsting lips
With water of your rain

When my eyes feast on your beauty
Giving the chartered wing
Of racing vibes and midnight thoughts
Of a day gone by
And dreaming of halcyon days to come

I long to share your dreams
Taste your lips and soul
Know the edges of paradise
Some where some day
On a giddy golden day
And know the raptured song of love

Missing You Tonight

I walk beside a still stream
Guided by a pale moon beam
Where a thousand booming frogs sing of gloom
And silent water bares it's bosom to the moon . . .

Arrow swift your voice comes by
Flung by a mad raptured night birds cry
Could a more poignant sorrow sing
In the great awakened spring . . . .

Fresh from sleep of winters rest
I looked into your sorrow crowded eyes
And saw your vision fade away
Into a hushed futile sky . . . .

So I search for you tonight my love
Let me fly beside a lonely dove
To waiting lips of crimson hue
Soft as rose petals, gentle as the morning dew . . .

I walk along in a misty shroud
My companion is a lonely cloud
That wandered across my lonely, lonely walk
And brought a gentle breeze to talk . . .

Of all your loveliness my sweet
And guide my troubled feet
To you—a pale star blushes in shame
When a gentle breeze calls your name . . .

How lovely, how beautiful I remember thee
With lovely face and spirit free
If this vision should fade with morning light
I will search the more for you tonight . . .

I Bought A Rose For You Today

I bought a rose for you today
I saw the roses flare
It caused my heart to sway
I chose a small and delicate one
For you, I bought a rose today
I could only pay the purchase price
As fire beauty was plucked from the stem
I handed the folded bills away
To a merchant with greedy hands
That yielded the rose I bought today
I looked at its fair beauty
Swelling tears came into my eyes
The rose bound by its duty
To speak, pleading anthems of love
Stalk plucked, it would die and lose its beauty
While red petals fall, no, are placed
Upon the milky white smoothness of your breast
There, the heaving breast would sway
And cause the flaming petals to blush in shame
I bought a rose for you today

The Sky and you

The evening sky was spent
Flung out over a blue gray horizon
It had said all that it would say
Streaked with tears of sorrow
Where flame and ash came to play . . .

Your memory, your face was etched in molten gray
Or was it framed in shades of flame
I saw the tilted impish nose and chin
On display in this broken sky
Then tears fell and pain cried from within . . .

Dear fading splendor sky
Sky of joy and sky of pain
Sky of many color traces
Sky of fading haunting memories
Sky of disappearing faces . . .

To Jan

31st Anniversary

How much do I love you
How many stars shine at night
How many waves lap the shore
If space continued seven times over
Could I possibly love you more . . .

How much do I love you
Ask me a million years from now
How soon the time flew by
While hand in hand we made our journey
From earth to startled sky . . .

How much—How much do I love you
Let me tell you on countless days
While the rainbow ends the mystic tears
That it would take to fill the seas
In a million passing years . . .

How much do I love you
The look, the touch, the smile
How much, baby, baby mine
In summer you are ice cubes
In winter you make the wine . . .

I will find you in a far flung sky
Where paths are strewn with gold
And silver leaves fall anew
When thunder echo's down life's valley
I Love you . . .
I Love you . . .
I Love you . . .

Two Wild Flowers

Two wild flowers grew
On a throbbing spring day
Atoms explode
Tossed by gentle wind and rain
They blushed, but knew no shame . . .

The whole spring long
They rejoiced in full blown beauty
Wild as throbbing pain
That exploded in the universe
With gifts of sun and rain . . .

Their cultured cousin graces
The shelves of elite florists
Midst cities roar and blight
And adorning fair ladies gowns
On a grand and pompous night . . .

Still the two wild flowers shared
A canopy of clouds of azure blue
And burst the shackled chains
Of a rainbow's brilliant hue . . .

But fading spring
Having kept her ritual
With pain and coming flame
Terminated her pregnancy
In a night that has no name . . .

And the two wild flowers
Looked in natures mirror
Saw fading splendor, fading beauty
And gave their shells back to earth
And claimed their shroud
And waited for another birth . . .

They knew no party gown
Nor graced a center piece
They listened to talking birds
And startled wing
And left their beauty on a far flung hill
To await another spring . . .

A Mans World

I hear it's a mans world
One that belongs to him
To carry the ball-or to hit it
While budding beauties stomp-jump
Surrender and cry at his heroic efforts

He builds empires, fortunes
Won and lost in a day-or a night
Molding other men to
Fit his needs, and to do his will

He builds homes, raises sons and daughters
Bears pain without a cry
Loathes weaker men
Follows stronger, for awhile

He is happy, he is in control
But then the loneliness of night sets in
And sounds soft and lonely cries
And the pain of memories begin
He built a kingdom for his queen
To share the sculptured throne
He gave commandments for the trumpets
To call her name alone

The king has lost his throne
Built with hands soft, strong and fragile
It is a mans world you know
Torn away by a woman's scorn

Fantasy Dreams

I took liberties with you last night
Of course you did not know
Cloaked behind my dreams
I took your body
Warm as the mid day sun
Your body, your passions too

There was a wild endless passion
While the stars kept
Their ritual in the sky
The clouds masked the moon in shame
In a night set aflame
By my own desire
Fueled by your fire
The night was ecstasy
Named by the night birds song

The morning came like vapor
And died with the chilling dawn
Dear lady,
Lady, that I know you to be
Please forgive me
For I am a mortal man
But I want you to know
Your privacy is sacred to me
And I would gladly give my life
To ensure that sanctity
Of precious womanhood
I alone am guilty
Of loosing my dreams in flight
Leaving my soul bared and lonely
Yet pleading for another night . . .

First Woman

"And the story begins"

Called Eve we are told
Created by breath of life and sod
By our Great Creator

What did she feel
and know
When she first knew
She was different from him
First man muscled and hard
Woman soft and yielding
To his searing look and questing hands
Blush on crimson cheeks
Parting lips that gasp
Twining arms that reach
And rise with body held-
Held taut
Welded by flames desire
To consume and mesh
Into one form
Yearning for seeking
A growing coming Pain

A Moonlit Night On My Lake Neptune Goddess

The moon was on my lake last night
The golden bar's overlapping
The wind blown waters
I watch this wealth with my eyes
Veiled and misty as the dawn
I knew you would come to me
Rising from
The insatiable bars of gold
Shimmering and shining
Teasing the minds of men
First I heard your voice

Transfixed, I searched the water's face
There I saw you, Neptune Goddess
Rising from the waters face
Shimmering, shining
Mirrored by the moon
Your stealthy movements flowed with grace
Bringing joy and passions flame
To your beautiful delicate face

For A Friend Who Is Lonely

I know you are walking
The paths of loneliness
Finding your way along
In a forest yet untrod
Reaching, searching, looking for a sign
Moss grows on the north side of trees
Mostly, but don't always
Count on it
Where, and what is North?
I pray that you will find
Peace and love
And beauty will return
Like the geese in springtime
I have felt your pain
And know some too
I hope, I pray you find the love
That will make you an endless day
Of joy and beauty
Followed by an eternal night of love

For every guy—For his special lady

Life is a mystery
It is a subtle thing
But sometimes in our mundane travels
We meet a kindred spirit
And part of the mystery unravels . . .

Where there is heat, there is flame
Flames sparked by some unknown god
Sparks that are kindled to a burning fire
As pagan throats roar out their lusty cry
Filled by insatiable pagan desires . . .

I know soft winds caress your skin
I see, I feel your warm beauty
You were created woman, I man
Could any chemist explain the force
That causes opposites to span . . .

The void that separates the two
Eyes and questing hands explore
And the universe burns bright
While sudden gasps and morning cries
Folds the burning day away for coming night . . .

Should I say more
Wasted words may fall on passing winds
And settle with the morning dew
Through time and circumstances
Can not erase the day
I touched your lips
And gained a paradise with you . . .

I will think of you

I will think of you
On wind swept mornings and evenings still
And long sad nights when eternity waits
To sing it's ceaseless song of love
In tune with the sorrow filled whippoorwill . . .

I will think of you
In evenings shadows ghostly maize
Of somber hues, gray mauve and dusty pink
When proud flitting fireflies
Prime the stars to blaze . . .

And spring will come
To break away the dead
To thaw the streams, to grant new birth
And fly the northern air stream
With honking geese,
Where haunting memories have fled . . . .

I will think of you
On halcyon days, in subtle ways
In mid day heat and early morning dew
When October days stir my gypsy feet
And hot blood pounds within my veins
When misty rain mingles with tears
I will think of you . . .

For lovers apart

I reached for your arms tonight
To feel your warm body next to mine
But you are not there
Gone—gone—gone away again
I searched for you in vain . . .

My lips, trembling, sought your full mouth
Warm as fire on a winters day
Oh my love, I could not feel your face
Or feel your sensitive embrace
Or touch the jet black hair . . .

We share this bed together
We know each other well
You are a lovely silhouette
In moon beams raptured silence
You dream away the night . . .

While you dream in silent slumber
Caressed by the watch of gods
Are you, could you dream of me
Reach for me, searching too
And hold my hand, my heart, my love . . .

Morning After

You make the coffee
Early in the morning
And bring me my cup
Along with yours
Crawl back in bed
After a while you will say
Sure wish I had some more coffee
My signal to rise and serve
After a night of love
Who could refuse
Half blind with sleep
I would pour
Which cup is yours
Oh I know
You always leave a little
In the bottom of your cup
Like a love offering to god
But mine all gone
Like a lusty pagan god
Consuming wine
We always were that way
I would burn all the candles
On a star splended night
You always held a little back
To brighten up
Another stormy blue black night

Actors

Life is a play
We act on its stage
Like stringed creatures
In a puppet show
Performing all the features . . .

We smile at hurt
And pull the quivering arrow
From our barren flesh
And soothe the stinging barbs
With gauze and tears that mesh . . .

We dry the tears
From a child's eye
And tell him big boys don't cry
And hide the ones on our own cheek
Strictly on the sly . . .

We tell oft-repeated stories
Around campfires at night
And wait our turn
For memories of other fires
And other nights return . . .

We dream in the night
With false bravado
And pagan heartbeats
That softly fades away
Like footsteps on a hollow street . . .

We dream of a perfect love
And learn too soon
That this mystical lady of our dreams
Is but an actress
Playing out her woven scenes . . .

We are lovers of the night
We are dreamers on a gilded stage
We are birds in flight
Flying to a distant sunset
Seeking solace in the night . . .

Actors

Life, you are a mysterious harlot
Selling favors to those who buy
You seldom ever give it
So we act on the stage of life
And I can't wait to live it . . .

Loves seasons

When did spring come? On a gray bleak day
When a sunbeam streaked across a tender sky
Or when the pagan gods saw your warm beauty
And unleashed their lusty cry . . .

On air currents for fragile wings to try
Spring came gushing, rushing new birth
Pushing at gray, dead lethargic sod
Singing raptured songs of merry mirth . . . .

My love you are spring, a red rose bud
Upon thorny vines, you give your kiss
To waft across the honey suckle vines
Where busy bees mix nectar with mornings magic mist

What is spring, what is it, tell me
Of dreams you dream, but would never tell
Dreams born in loves secret nook
Where cupid casts a magic spell
Yes my love, you are spring
You are spring . . . .

How did summer come? On a warm torrid day
When the night birds sing their ceaseless song
And fire flies build their fragile flames
To tease the minds of men in twilight sarongs . . .

You are summer love, sweet and fragrant
As lotus blossoms in perfumed hair
When the flesh pains of enraptured man
Fall captive to your secret lair . . .

If a captive I must become
No longer valiant and free
Will you capture me with your web of love
Woven with feminine intricacy
You are summer love
You are summer . . .

When will fall come love
In subtle ways, on haughty days
When wind wolves sing mad raptured mournful songs

Loves seasons

And holly hills flame with natures blaze . . .
And gypsy blood is stirred
To become a pulsing living thing
While the conductor of all this
Prepares my heart to sing . . .

Of all your tranquil beauty
Where every hill is torched in fame
Where the wind unmasks the clouds
To see their blushing shame . . .

Oh blue and infinite tender sky
Send to me a dove of unblemished fame
To fly straight to this awaiting heart
To speak to me and call gently your name . . .

What sweet memories I have of fall
When the jack-o-lantern moon casts its glow
To warm away the frost bite
Like fire in early winters snow
You are fall my sweet
You are fall . . . .

Dreary winter I do not care to think of thee
Should love passions die and freeze
Like a red-hot ember in icy veins
I'll think instead of springs coming breeze . . .

If I could write a love song for you

If I could write a love song for you
I would write it beneath the stars
And all the stars of night
Would shine upon my pages
Bathing them in soft flowing light

If I could write a love song for you
It would be by a softly running brook
And misty fragrance of blooming flowers
Would sweeten the mystical air
Roses, jasmine honey suckle
To gladden this happy hour

The poets would bow their heads in shame
When the love song called your name
Myriad's of nightingales would sing
The whole night long
To keep the endless lovers vows
Flowing, growing, throbbing in the song

If I could write a love song for you
It would be by a meadow still
With the sound of silence all around
My pounding heart would not be still
When thoughts of you abound

And when it is finished
I will beg of a wounded bird
A little sparrow with a broken wing
To deliver it to you
Ah, you could not refuse to sing

And heal the sparrow's broken wing
To see it fly away
Into the heavens, healed and free
While I, beggar that I am
Waiting on bended knee

Would ask, trembling, waiting
Could your love song
Does you love song
Born of spirit free
Even possibly mention me

Haunting eyes

Some star studded moon beamed
Fire brilliant night
When loves caress is fire drum hot
And molten lava cools from loves respite . . .

Oh, if you should come to me
In one sweet savage desire
And give yourself to me
To quench my raging fire . . .

Then you would unloose the shackle
That binds and imprisons me
Your lips would let my heart take wings
And soar in flight like winds blown free . . .

But should you go your way
And take your smile from me
Then your memory would linger
In my mind constantly . . .

The stars and moon, no longer bright
The mountains would diminish in size
For I have become captive
To your doe like haunting eyes . . .

So you hold the keys
To my heart strings door
On a brilliant blue black night
Will I hear silence or fire drums roar . . .

I would posses your sweetness
And long to hear your sighs
And feel your heart beat throbs
So speaks a captive
Of doe like haunting eyes . . .

Bouquet—alive—dead

You brought me flowers today my love
All colors of the flaming sky
They were your disguise
For sad and tender eyes . . .

In the spring you brought the rose
Tender bud and delicate stem
Swelling with growing passion
Overflowing at its red tipped brim . . .

In summer you brought a marigold
Mature and full in all its grace
Its full blown beauty
Was mirrored by your lovely face . . .

In winter you brought poinsettias
The red tipped one to pierce my heart
The white to seal icy veins
Left cold by its stinging dart . . .

Yes, today you brought me flowers
Spring warm and summers searing kiss
Growing cold in autumns fading splendor
Dying in winters cold gray mist . . .

If

If I could only be
What you wanted me to be
To change in the twinkling of an eye
Perhaps you would stay
And never say goodbye

If I could only see
What you wanted me to see
Reach down into the blindness of my heart
And walk your well meaning path
Perhaps we would never part

If I could only know
What you wanted me to know
About your needs hurts and pain
Then I could always love you
And never break your heart again

If I could only share
What you wanted me to share
And kiss the hurt and cares away
And let you draw from my strength
To keep the empty nights away

Wind messages

The wind came again today
It frolicked through the falling leaves
It sped a goose home south in flight
It brought a chill across my spine
It moaned in sorrow in the night . . .

The wind was restless again today
Not content to let still waters lie
It moved with awkward grace
Pushing the surging foam
To a-new and changing place . . .

The wind came again today
Following the path of night
It blew some sparks to flame
It broke my heart anew
For the wind has called your name . . .

To a dreamer

A soft muted violin crying in the night
Like a thousand broken souls imprisoned
Trying to escape
Reaching for freedoms outer bounds
Touching, moving, reaching, guiding all other sound . . .

While violins cry, cello's sob
In rhythm with the drums pulsing beat
And dulcet tones of saxophones

A palace orchestra in regal attire
The conductor poised in anticipation
While chandeliers gleam in brilliant splendor
Polished marble adds it's charm
All await the Queen . . .

Then a vision flows across the ballroom floor
Every eye and soul glides with her
Enraptured, captured by the queens' flowing gown
Regal crown—incomparable beauty . . .

The queen dances the night away
Heart beats sway and throb, aching to share the throne
When dawn comes, on silent misty wings
My soul cries out for the queen, but the vision is gone
Gone . . . gone . . . gone . . .

Choosing

Spring has exploded upon the earth
Virile crested flowers frame the soil
While soul and spirit blush in shame

The skies have dumped their pregnant waters
Where electric fingers gashed the
Startled frame swollen earth gave birth

I walk among the torrid reds
And peek at the blushing rose
Prick the thorny vines

Which will I choose
For a bouquet for my love
Where and what is the name

Who can name the flowers
Who has the right to break the stem
That separates life from life

Once I brought a bouquet
With fever in the night
Afterwards I wished the flowers re-stalked
I bend my back my hand to reach
For the flower of my choice
A red, a gold, a rose

I cannot pick
I cannot choose
I come empty to you in the night
Tell me I did the right thing, love
There is no bouquet for you
Only flesh and joy and pain

And after it is finished
Frail choices remain
And I have given the flower its name

The earth for its basket
The sky for its cover
My bed for its shame

A day like this

Wasn't it a day like this
When the sky was perfect azure blue
Not a cloud to mar the tranquil bliss
Or break the magic spell
Of your tender loving kiss . . . .

I remember it was a day
When thin golden threads
Traced across the gauze
Of time then held the moments rapture
And caused eternity to pause . . .

Did an eagle scream
Across a deathless valley
Tearing out its chilling cry
While I—I did not hear a murmur
Or see the swelling tear in your eye . . . .

I know, I do remember
That I was caught in a gauzy web
Of love and splintered bliss
I have catalogued the days in memory
Wasn't it a day like this . . .

The Last Poem

I shall never read
Nor write
The last poem in a book
For poets speak
And cry and share
And I with those
Whose hearts have bled
Will always know
There are so many things
I could, and should have said

Saved for the
Last Poem

Love Thoughts 2

Curtain Calls

Deserts burn
And mountains freeze
While gentle winds caress
Your hair, your eyes, your lips
Slowly parting, whispers yes . . .

Mornings explode
And twilight shadows creep
To await a rising pastel moon
That greets a lonely nightingales'
Sad and mournful tune . . .

Singing of a night of passion
While shooting stars pass by
And the night steals softly away
Leaving lovers gaunt taut nerves
To greet the sad and lonely day . . .

Mornings wane
And evenings come
While silent curtains fall
On shrouded stage
Where lovers wait for curtain calls . . .

Understanding

If I could share with you
Just one moment in time
Let it not be with a kiss or a hug
Or a wasted word
Let us in passing
Share the one moment
When we glance
And each would know
The
  Other
      Understood . . .

My Shadow

In the long misty night
Chiseled out of ebony
Where dark etchings gather
No, collide
With sinister fetchings
Of time and place

You came down that long narrow corridor
Warmed by angelic light
Surrounded by warm vibrations
To take the chill from the night

For a moment you owned the night
Then you disappeared in the strangled light
Gone, gone, gone, from my view
Let my spirit find and envelop you
Let my shadows soft fringes
Surround you, and keep you safe . . . .

We'd Make Love

Sometimes I think you want me
And with that macho mind of mine
I think we will make love till dawn
But the raging fire consumes
To burning embers, ashes and yawn's

Afterwards I say, don't touch my body
You don't know me that well
You give me a kick and yell
That was good lovin'

I grow quiet
Tar baby, he don't say nothing
And the long full pull of the gentle glow
Of soft gentle vibes
That fall in easy ebb and flow

We'd make love
In the secret annals of our hearts
And seal the eternal quest
Of limb thigh and tongue
Waiting, saving the last for best

I guess you know I want you
And wonder how you feel tonight
And gentle, no racing blood will tell
And cause this macho mind and body
To ask the throbbing question—
Could we make love . . .

Come To See Me In The Spring

When the short gray days are past
And winters cold is gone at last
When the last icicle is gone
When I am feeling so alone
Come and see me in the spring

When the swelling life breaks the sod
Pushes and breaks the heavy clod
Of clay, sprinkled with rain
And I need a balm for pain
Come and see me in the spring

When the red birds sing their song
And all god's creatures join the throng
To sing anthems to celebrate life
When a vibrant soul sheds strife
Come and see me in the spring

When my gentle eyes shed tears
And my soul is full of fears
When the rose is no longer dead
Make a bouquet pink, white, yellow, and red
And Come to see me in the spring

Illusions

The night was a fragment
Of a mans fantasies and dreams
In the quiet semi darkness
You did your dance
No, it was a gift
Of perfumed flesh
Veiled in soft folds
Of transparent cloth

I saw your nakedness
And the stars exploded
From the heavens
Revealing a tawny body
With perfect delicate breasts
And sensuous undulating hips
That drove me wild
With ecstasy and pain
Later I would feed your hungry body
Your insatiable body

Would drown the fire from my own yearning flesh
The dance consummated
Into a mans quest for a woman
She the tempest, the tease
He the conqueror, the strong
Flexing muscles
Brought to a quiver
By your untamed innocence
Your strength
Greater than my own
I remember a night scene
And long for it's return

A Christmas gift

If I give you a diamond
On Christmas day
Do not think
It truly expresses my love
For that is found only
In the rushing truth
Of a moment
When I have seen your love
Expressed
In the many things you do
Cooking, cleaning, washing
You open the door
That is closed
Like an unopened Christmas present
Waiting to be opened
When I come home
From a long weary day

Spring love

Our love grew vibrant in the spring
It burst forth from the sod of flesh
Tearing away the weary crust
To become a pulsing living thing . . .

It flamed with the icy winds of March
And grew warm with April showers
Touched by the tears of May
That brings forth the brilliant flowers . . . .

Spring is fresh—alive and new
It brings a kiss on gentle wings
Given by a soft full lovely mouth
That whispers love, and starts the stars to sing . . .

Lonely Lady-Lonely Man

There is a lonely lady
In a quiet and lonely town
She is a lovely beauty
Quietly performing her duties

The day goes slowly by
Drifting quietly into the night
The dying sun has set
She takes care of her families' needs
Leaving her own needs unmet

The evening is quiet and lonely
Doing a working wife's evening chores
Cooking-cleaning
How soon the evening passes
Leaving her arms searching, reaching

For after all the lights go out
And she curls up all alone
She reaches, reaches, groping
For a love that is gone, gone, gone
Her heart is seeking, searching, hoping

There is a lonely lady
In a quite and lonely town
And longs for love throughout the night
Rising with broken sorrow
At dawns early light

There is a lonely man
In a quiet and lonely town
One star filled night
The lonely lady will meet the lonely man
And make love till the early mornings light

The whole night long
While tender moon beams embrace the stars

And all the God's grand
Tremble when the lonely lady makes love with the lonely man

Servant Messenger

Stark against the gray dark mountains
A lonely windmill moans its song
To the canopied slopes below
Singing an eternal love song
Singing soft and low . . .

This raw rugged canyon
Is my mistress this morning
Its inhabitants cling to me
Like the love of a beautiful woman
That will never set me free . . .

The cactus with its thorns and hooks
Sets deep in the flesh of man
Leaving an indelible mark
A tiny scar, a crimson spot
The pain is not equal to the spank . . .

Of love ignited
On another halcyon day
By a tremoring voice
blown freely by a careless voice
leaving me a haunting choice . . .
Love a spirit
Blown freely by the wind
Love a tender beautiful voice
Love a beautiful lady
My heart leaves me no choice . . .

This canyon is my mistress
My servant, myriads of song birds
Proclaiming my love to one this day
They speed my throbbing message
To a lady far away . . .

A Summer Rain

The day is hot
The Texas sun spares no one
Hot, dry, hot, humid
But there are no clouds
Gathering in a listless sky

A breeze starts to stir
The cool refreshing rain
Splashes on my upturned face
To taste the rain on my waiting hungry lips
Refreshing me
But soon the rain is gone
Leaving the mysteries of life
Fading with the passing clouds

You were like that
You came at a time
When I could not help but want you
The days were hot and long
Passing away into an un-passing night
You came like a summer rain
And when you were through
Refreshing my tongue
And pouring your raindrops
Over my aching body
I was renewed for awhile
But soon you were gone
Leaving the mysteries of the
Universe entangled ever more
And the roots of my soul
Thirsting, crying out for more . . .

A Love Song For Thee

More beautiful than the morning sun
Sweeter than the morning mist
I implored a song bird free
To sing my love song
To sing only for thee

Thrice more beautiful than the stars
Mauve, gold, and cobalt blue
The little bird grew in pride
It sang with all it's might
Putting all its cares aside

It burst its throbbing throat
It sang to the morning sun
To wane with the rising moon
All of god's creations
Were enraptured by its tune

It sang beneath your windowsill
Throbbing, quivering, singing
My love song questions to you
Do you love me, do you love me
You answer softly I do, I do . . . .

Gray In Your Hair

You've mentioned it to me before
How you wish it wasn't there
Do not change, do not touch
The beauty of your hair

It is a mark of dignity
Having passed some milestones
It proves (if you need proving)
You're a winner in my mind

You watched your children grow
Cradled, nurtured them through
Sickness, growing pains
They are a mirror of you

You gave them your all
You still do, mothers are like that
They cherish and honor you

You had it tough when you were a kid
I know because you have told me
But, I know you grew up strong
Loving, caring, a real woman to be
I hear strength in your voice
I hear needs unmet too
I long to touch your pretty gray hair
Because it belongs to you . . . .

Will you love me

Will you love me
When the fires of life have died
Will you love me
When I call you too much
And say all the wrong things

Will you love me
When I repeat the same asked questions
And find you unaware
That I am talking to you
Listening too
And saying to you, I care

Will you love me when
I am not cool or suave
Or maybe someday need a toupee
When the times seem so bad
And I need your strength to lean on

Will you love me with passions flame
Or let me lay quietly in bed with you
Will you love me with no holds barred
And hold nothing back
Will you love me freely
And give yourself to me
Will you love this unique personality, me!

There Will Never Be Enough Time

There will never be enough time
To tell you how much I love you
For it to be branded
Into your heart and mind
So that you really know
How much I need you
And just how much I care

There is never enough time
To capture your attention
And to speak of your beauty fair
To whisper the things of love
That the rising moon
Could only blush about

Song birds will form a chorus
Carried on the soft footsteps
Of a gentle wind
The stars will twinkle when I call your name
And dance across the brittle sky
Tenderly, lest they break the spell
Of the enchanted night

There will never be enough time
To think of the impossible moment
When I first heard your voice
And all the moments of time stood still
While my heart raced ahead
And words could only come
Slowly to my trembling lips

Given the improbabilities
Of your earthly path crossing mine
I can only thank whatever
Gods that be
For your path that crosses mine
And know with all assurance
There will never be enough time
To love you

Maybe past this life
When rushing winds charge
Down corridors of long past memories
The wind will brush back

There Will Never Be Enough Time

The pages of life
And find me still
Searching for enough time with you

I will

I will go softly with the wind
Churning, soothing cooling
Giving zest to life with flair
We will seek you out
And blow gently through your hair

I will go with the falling rain
Bringing miracles to earth
The flowers will ever explode
And I will be a tiny raindrop
And settle gently on your nose

I will rise with the morning light
Climbing the endless stairs
Of space and the morning sun
Shining on giddy days of March
To catch you on the run

I will go with the fading light
To finish the day at last
Laying aside all earthly sorrow
Giving back to the finished day
Anything you have borrowed
I will come with the first
Bright star of evening time
To settle the stars in place
We will make a mirror of muted lights
To touch your lips and face

I will come with an evening prayer
And fold you in the dreams
Of magic sleep
I will watch you through the night
And pray you never weep

I will find you now
And always love
Should you travel far
Should mystic rain leave your hair
I will borrow moonbeams
On a tranquil lake
And send you gifts
Of golden bars

I Have Tried To Lose Your Face

I have tried at least
A thousand times to lose your face
Embedded deep in the fibers of my mind
I try, I cannot forget
Nor can I embrace
The thought of losing you
I hear your voice so often
I remember the past
Not always in person or on the phone
But mostly in the melodies of my heart

Sometimes I cry the stars to sleep
And whisper gently to the clouds
They alone will know
The sorrows that have passed my lips
Anthems that roll down the churning clouds
Of a wasted sky

But yet I search for
That same glorious face
In a blushing hint of sunrise
And the long haunting cry of a whippoorwill
In a dying purple sky
I try to lose your face

If You Were

If you were a rain drop
I know it would be soft and gentle
If you were a rain storm
You would soak the barren soil
And give it new life

If you were a snowflake
You would be unique in all the world
As every snowflake is
You would cover the winter trees with white
And I would cry out with delight

If you were a rainbow
And I was found at the end
Searching for you
I would not search for gold
But for your beauty fair

If you were mine
And you may be soon
Then my heart will soar with eagles
Screaming out across the heavens vast
And all the pains of the world
Will be wiped away at last

If you were a beggar
I would find you loaves of bread
Brush your matted hair
And wipe away the pain from your feet
Then put you on a queenly throne
Your Royal Highness

You Have A Friend

You have a friend
When the night is cold
My love, hot as burning embers
Will keep you warm and safe
In January nights and Decembers

You have a friend
When others have passed you by
And thrown scorn your way
When the cold chilling dawn
Breaks into a long haunting day

You have a friend
And you can shed your tears
Upon my face and chest
When your heart beats
It can seek its own requests

You have a friend
When others say you are wrong
It matters not to me
To take your side against the world
To make you strong and free
I cannot say
When it all began
Or even how it will end
But I do know this
You will, you do, have a friend

Tears at Dawn

I walked the silent hills this morning
Searching, looking for you
I walked along grassy slopes
Where my tears mingled with morning dew . . .

I searched the dawns first faint rays
Looking into a fractured sky
Remembering your beautiful
Misty shrouded eyes . . .

And how once they sparkled
When they looked into my own
Under soft chestnut curls
All tossed about and wind blown . . .

Yes I looked for you this morning
Searching, searching in sorrow my love
And somewhere I heard your voice
In the cooing of a dove . . .

And then there was silence
On this fresh virgin day
Where I left bitter tears
On the path where you walked away . . .

There in the silent dawn
Where I walked with memories of you
Remembering somehow eased the heartache
Where I left tears mingled with dew . . .

You did not come to me today my love
But I know you will by and by
The sun will burst forth
To dry up a tear dampened sky . . .

Roses for sale

Roses, roses, Sir-roses for sale
Sale by one or two or more
Roses, beautiful roses for sale
Roses, dark and mysterious
Roses, soft and pale

I looked at the gathered roses
To choose one for my love

The soft delicate pinks
With petals soft as god's first morning
Forming soft delicate links

The yellow one's appealed to me
With splattered slabs of gold
Its veins held great riches no man could know
Banks could not hold its treasures
Its bins would over flow

The white roses were pure as winters first snow
Its purity beckoned to me
Fresh as morning cream
It makes me remember
Soft and gentle scenes

Then the red rose blushed in shame
Warm as the evening sun
Its red passions shone through
It is my choice of roses love
To prove my love for you . . . .

Two Hearts

Two hearts beat
With the same thud
That sends life
Exploding into the bodies
Of a man and woman

Two hearts need healing
Where the soul joins that
Same rhythmic ebb and flow
I see your heart is broken
I can tell by the beauty
That was once there
That has faded into
A sorrowed sunset
Let me fix your heart
The best way I know how

I would start by showing you the stars
And claiming a small planet for you
I would add an island
Set in tranquil seas
So your Neptune spirits
Would hear all the voices of the seas
I know you have that physic power

I would find a mountain
To return to when you tire
Of hearing the wailing winds
I would find a peaceful valley
With a mystic brook running through
With a veiled house in
The distant shadows
Colored in mauve veils
And soft cinnabar and song birds
All about . . .

I would find a palace for you
With white tigers by a lotus pool
And black tawny leopards too
And servants of the mind
To do your will

I would add the laughter
Of your children

Two Hearts

To complete your perfect symphony
Graced and blessed by the
Soft clinging sounds of
Wind chimes, nursery rhymes
Fixed hurts and midnight
Thoughts of love return
As for me

I would ask you
To do your magic healing
With your love potions
Mixed with laughter, joy
And giving yourself to me
You will know what to do
And two hearts mended now
Will beat through eternity
As one

Little bird, you're free

You are a whippoorwill
Crying in the night
All that is mournful
Calling out to the long dark shadows

You are a mourning dove
Calling its haunting song
Of love and remorse
Across an endless field of dreams and beauty

You are a cockatoo
With outrageous sun streaked beauty
Preened and proud
You are the gentle sparrow
Singing its quiet song
In a voice soft and gentle

You are the swan
Kissed by grace and beauty
Cloaked in angelic white

I have loosed your wings
To fly the air streams
Swift and free
You could never live in captivity
Dying in life's mysteries

Now your wings will take you
Where ever you want to go
Across the lands
Across the seas
But little bird, should you grow weary
And life treats you unkindly
Come with the spring
And rebuild you nest in my tree . . .

Look at me

Look at this face
I know the lines there
Like a well-read road map
I know it shows miles
And miles of travel through life

Look at these hands
I know they are callused
And past the age of beauty
They have known hard times
And long, long hours of hard work

Look at this body
Mr. America it's not
Or a "hunk" as they say
It certainly won't win
A body builders contest

But look at this face again
Look at the gleam in my eye
When I look upon you with love
Not seeing a blemish
On your face or countenance
Look at the joy and
Energy shown in life

Look at these hands
Feel them as they touch and caress you
Like a lover of fine paintings
Touching a priceless piece of art
Or touching a child so gently
Only to hold and love so tenderly

Feel this body loving you
Not as youthful as it once was
But stronger and wiser
And more knowing
Of a woman's needs
And more able to love you better

She loves me—She loves me not

Wild flowers grow
On a fine promising day
Reds and pinks yellow too
They held tranquil beauty
And frolicked when the
Gentle winds blew them to play

A sunflower ripe in beauty
Beautiful yellows
And a center brown
I plucked its petals to know
If you love me
Or if she loves me not
I always cheated a little
To make sure she loved me

A buttercup on the way to school
Its yellow nectar held
In a delicious cup of beauty
Hold it under the chin
Of the girl you love
If her chin is yellow stained
When the cup is removed
It means you can kiss her
Wow, it means I can kiss you

Does it really give me the right
Can I kiss you please
I'll go for a dozen buttercups
To stain your chin
Now when I start to kiss you
Please don't sneeze

You and I

You are the warm rays of sunshine
You are the moonbeams of night time
You are my constant thought
You are my anytime

I know you will be my springtime
I will feel your warmth in summertime
I will harvest your love in fall
I cannot think of wintertime

You are springs gentle touch
I know I will love you very much
When you touch my hair of autum
And caress and kiss and touch

Down past where blood and sinew go
Past the throbbing aching glow
Of passions real and warm
Past heartbeats wild throbbing flow

I will cry out in the empty night
Sometimes when your not there
I'll call to you in mental waves
And you'll call back, I CARE

And some lonely nights we'll share passion
When we're really apart, alone
I'll touch your aching body
And you'll answer with your moans

I heard your voice today

I heard your voice today
It came in soft gentle vibe's
It rode the wind with ease
Calling back the haunting memories
To laugh and cry and tease

I heard your voice today
I stood on a mountaintop
And thundered your name so free
Down the waiting eager canyon
And it echoed back to me

I heard your voice today
As I stood by the ocean shore
I cast your name to the roaring sea
How soon the thunderous roar
Brought your name crashing back to me

I heard your name again today
It was carried by a silent voice
Inside the depths of me
It came in remembered scenes
And it was good to be so near thee

And my faithful friends of the air
Honking, making their pilgrimage home
Brought your name along in their flight
And I listened, trembling, throbbing
As your name drifted away
Into the night

The Night

When the last fleeting shadows
Of fading light
Have passed their way
And night sweet night
Surround my soul
And binds my inner most thoughts
To its bosom
It is the night
Holding soft lamp lights glow
That brings remembered scenes
In easy ebb and flow

It is the night
Some broken, some serene
As I lay quietly the whole night through
Sharp arrows pierced my soul
Leaving indelible thoughts of you

It is the night
That brought you in my arms
And the stars exploded
At once as one
In the fractured heavens
The Milky Way danced
For enthralled lovers
To see

And ask for encores
More and more and more

It is the night
That brought your warm body to me
Scent of roses, Jasmine too
On perfumed flesh
And all the flowers of paradise
Bloomed in you
Touching my quivering nostrils
Through the night
Given to me by you

I can not see
I can not feel
The tearing pain of light
For I have an anesthetic balm

The Night

Given in gentle doses by you
It is the night
THE NIGHT

The Last Poem

I shall never read
Nor write
The last poem in a book
For poets speak
And cry and share
And I with those
Whose hearts have bled
Will always know
There are so many things
I could, and should have said

Saved for the
Last Poem